Early Childhood Teacher Education
Part-Time Program
Class of 2012

Rudolf Steiner Centre Toronto

Carly Wilson

SPIRITUAL INSIGHTS
VOLUME 2 of THE LITTLE SERIES
First English Printing, 1999
Second English Printing, 2004
by the Waldorf Early Childhood
Association of North America, Inc.

Originally published in German
by the Internationale Vereinigung der
Waldorfkindergärten e.V., Stuttgart, as
DIE KLEINIE REIHE, NR1.GEISTIGE GABEN,
AUGUST 1996.

TO ORDER, CONTACT:
Waldorf Early Childhood Association
285 Hungry Hollow Road
Spring Valley, NY 10977
(845) 352-1690
FAX (845) 352-1695
Email info@waldorfearlychildhood.org
ISBN# 0-9722238-2-7 Volume 2

Dear Colleagues in the International Waldorf Movement,
and in particular, the Kindergartens,

In 1984, the International Waldorf Kindergarten Association came together for a conference in Dornach for the first time. The first version of this booklet was prepared for a seminar at that conference. The seminar was entitled, "Spiritual Gifts for the Educator." That first edition was followed by a second, unrevised edition for use in the training of teachers and in the continuing education of teachers. After seven years this expanded and revised third edition appeared as part of the Little Series of booklets published by the International Kindergarten Vereinigung. The foreword from the 1984 edition still applies today. It reads:

Our work on behalf of children takes place against the background of the increasingly dramatic spiritual struggles of our time. There is confusion in judgments regarding spiritual and non-spiritual streams. There is confusion that goes right into the question of personal destiny and into matters of the social forms needed to deal with the demands made of us. Where will we find the sources for our strength?

Out of our work with Rudolf Steiner's study of the human being, out of our work with exercises, meditations and prayers, an inner decisiveness can grow and the forces of love can arise, which we need for our daily work.

Some of the gifts for the inner path, arising from Rudolf Steiner's spiritual research, from the Christ-filled heart realm, are presented here for your use. They are creators of love, giving strength and trust, and opening spiritual expanses. Through them we will always know ourselves to be connected with one another over great distances of space and time.

With my whole heart, I wish teachers and parents may discover the sources of strength that stream from the words of Rudolf Steiner, "Inner exercise frees us and strengthens us for our tasks with the children, together with the parents, together with our colleagues."

Helmut Von Kügelgen, August 1966
Stuttgart, Dornach and Wilton, New Hampshire

Preface to the First English Edition

This English translation was first prepared for a workshop at an international Waldorf kindergarten conference held in Wilton, New Hampshire in August 1996. If these passages by Rudolf Steiner have already been printed, their sources are identified. Much has not been previously translated or was written for this publication.

In this new century, life grows ever more intense. One answer to the stress of the times is to clear a space for inner work and make it a regular part of one's life. A few minutes a day to focus on the essential aspects of life and to build up inner capacities helps enormously in meeting the challenging situations that face us.

Rudolf Steiner's work is full of indications and exercises to help one on the path of inner development. We are extremely grateful to Dr. Helmut von Kügelgen for compiling this booklet, so full of wonderful gifts, and we are happy to make it available to an English speaking audience.

On 25 February 1998, Helmut von Kügelgen crossed the threshold of death at age eighty-one. Originally a journalist, he became a Waldorf class teacher in Stuttgart and took four classes through the original Waldorf school. He was also a religion teacher and was very devoted to the development of the free religion lessons and services in Waldorf schools around the world. As he approached retirement in the 1970s, he began to concentrate his attention on the needs of the young children and the many ways that childhood was coming under attack. He became the leader of the International Waldorf Kindergarten Association and of the Kindergarten Seminar in Stuttgart. In these positions, he inspired thousands of kindergarten teachers around the world.

At kindergarten conferences in Europe, I had the privilege — and the challenge — of translating Dr. von Kügelgen's lectures into English. When he spoke of meditative content, whether the Foundation Stone, the Rose Cross meditation, or other exercises, he so beautifully spoke out of the spirit of the content, that translating the words alone did not suffice. I realized I too needed to work with the same meditative content if I was to do justice to his talks. Many of the verses and words that he drew upon for inspiration were gathered together in the German version of this booklet, and working with it became an intimate part of my own spiritual work. We make this volume and others in the Little Series available now, following his death, as a special gift to him.

Many people have helped bring this English version to completion and we would like to express special thanks to Alice Trembour who did much of the translating and editing, to Lydia Roberson who prepared the book for publication, to Fred Paddock and Judith Soleil of the Rudolf Steiner Library for their wonderful help in tracking down English translations, Dale Hushbeck for the new design concept, Sandy Littell for the graphic design and book production, Jorge Sanz Cordona for the cover art, and to the various publishers and translators whose work made this edition possible.

A Note on Translation

Rudolf Steiner commonly used the word "Mensch" when referring to the human being. In German, this word embraces both man and woman. When it was translated into English, the world "man" was usually used, which in common usage omits the feminine. We have often replaced this with "human being" or "humanity," but in some places this does not work well. In such instances, we have used the word "Man" and ask the reader to understand the word in its original sense of embracing man and woman.

Joan Almon,
Michaelmas 1998

A Note from the Publisher

In this second printing of *SPIRITUAL INSIGHTS*, we have updated the excerpts to include the most recent published translations wherever possible. Our thanks to Lydia Roberson, Melissa Lyons, and Naomi Olsen for their additional work. A special thanks to Judith Soleil and Judith Kiely of the Rudolf Steiner Library for her wonderful help in researching sources for many of the verses.

Susan Howard,
Waldorf Early Childhood Association
of North America, January 2004

✦ From *AWAKENING TO COMMUNITY*, 23 January 1923, Dornach and Stuttgart,
Lecture 1, Anthroposophic Press, 1974, p. 6.

Anthroposophical ideas are vessels
Fashioned by love,
and Man's being is spiritually summoned by the spiritual world
to partake of their content.
Anthroposophy must bring the light of true humanness
to shine out in thoughts that bear love's imprint;
knowledge is only the form
in which the human being reflects the possibility of receiving
in his or her heart
the light of the world spirit that has come to dwell there
and from that heart illuminate human thought.
Since real Anthroposophy cannot be grasped
except by the power of love,
it is love-engendering
when human beings take it in a way true to its own nature.

Meditative Words Which Seize the Will

Victorious Spirit
Flame through the impotence of irresolute Souls,
Burn out the egoism,
Ignite the compassion,
That selflessness,
The life stream of mankind,
Well up as the source
Of Spirit rebirth.

Foundation Stone Verse

for the First Additional Building of the Waldorf School

✦ in Stuttgart, 16 December 1921. Reprinted in TOWARDS THE DEEPENING OF WALDORF EDUCATION, Pedagogical Section of the School of Spiritual Science, Goetheanum, 1991, p. 124.

May there reign here spirit-strength in love;
May there work here spirit-light in goodness;
Born from certainty of heart,
And from steadfastness of soul,
So that we may bring to young human beings
Bodily strength for work,
Inwardness of soul,
And clarity of spirit.

May this place be consecrated to such a task;
May young minds and hearts here find
Servers of the light, endowed with strength,
Who will guard and cherish them.

Those who here lay the stone as a sign
Will think in their hearts of the spirit
That should reign in this place,
So that the foundation may be firm
Upon which there shall live and weave and work:
Wisdom that bestows freedom,
Strengthening spirit-power,
All-revealing spirit-life.

This we wish to affirm
In the name of Christ
With pure intent
And with good will:

(Then follow names)

The founding of Waldorf education took place on 21 August 1919 at the beginning of the first lecture of *THE FOUNDATIONS OF HUMAN EXPERIENCE*, originally published as *STUDY OF MAN*, (GA 293), Anthroposophic Press, 1996. In a "prayerful way," Rudolf Steiner set forth the relationship between those who wish to be active in our education and the Beings of the Third Hierarchy: with the Spirit of time, the Spirits of community destiny, and the higher self of each individual — the Archai, the Archangels and the Angels. There followed sixteen days of intensive work out of which these basic principles arise.

The fourteenth lecture of *THE FOUNDATIONS OF HUMAN EXPERIENCE* closes with a motto for the educator by Rudolf Steiner:

The need for imagination, a sense of truth, a feeling for responsibility, these are the three forces that are the nerves of education. And all those who want to take up the pedagogy must commit themselves to this motto before approaching the education:
Permeate yourself with the power of imagination.
Have courage for the truth.
Sharpen your feeling for responsibility of soul.

Day by day, Rudolf Steiner accompanied the *THE FOUNDATIONS OF HUMAN EXPERIENCE* with fourteen lectures about *PRACTICAL ADVICE TO TEACHERS* (GA 294) and with *DISCUSSIONS WITH TEACHERS* (GA 295, 21 August – 6 September 1919, Stuttgart, Anthroposophic Press, 1997).

On 6 September he closed the inauguration of Waldorf pedagogy — or the art of education — with three lectures on the curriculum as well as the fifteenth seminar discussion. In his closing words Rudolf Steiner gave four additional principals for every teacher and educator and, at the very end, recalled the beginning, the relationship to the spiritual world. (The indications for teachers are taken from the closing words of the series *DISCUSSIONS WITH TEACHERS*, pp. 164-166.)

Today I would like to conclude this discussion by pointing out something I want to lay upon your heads — that I would like you to stick firmly to the following four principles.

First, teachers must make sure that they influence and work on their pupils, in a broader sense, by allowing the spirit to flow through their whole being as teachers, and also in the details of their work: how each word is spoken, and how each concept or feeling is developed. Teachers must be people of initiative. They must be filled with initiative. Teachers must never be careless or lazy; they must, at every moment, stand in full consciousness of what they do in the school and how they act toward the children. This is the first principle. The teacher must be a person of initiative in everything done, great and small.

Second, my dear friends, we as teachers must take an interest in everything happening in the world and in whatever concerns humankind. All that is happening in the outside world and in human life must arouse our interest. It would be deplorable if we as teachers were to shut ourselves off from anything that might interest human beings. We should take an interest in the affairs of the outside world, and we should also be able to enter into anything, great or small, that concerns every single child in our care. That is the second principle. The teacher should be one who is interested in the being of the whole world and of humanity.

Third, the teacher must be one who never compromises in the heart and mind with what is untrue. The teacher must be true in the depths of being. Teachers must never compromise with untruth, because if they did, we would see how untruth would find its way through many channels into our teaching, especially in the way we present the subjects. Our teaching will only bear the stamp of truth when we ardently strive for truth in ourselves.

And now comes something more easily said than done, but it is, nevertheless, also a golden rule for the teacher's calling. The teacher must never get stale or grow sour. Cherish a mood of soul that is fresh and healthy! No getting stale and sour! This must be the teacher's endeavor.

Let us especially keep before us the thought, which will truly guide our hearts and minds, that connected with the present day spiritual movement are also the spiritual powers that guide the cosmos. When we believe in these good spiritual powers they will inspire our lives and we will truly be able to teach. To be free, independent artists of education and tenders of humanity as educators and teachers, this is what Rudolf Steiner wished for us. The three lecture cycles are full of impulses and insight into the nature and development of the human being: Think back on all we have done, and there will come to you, in general, thoughts about arrangements, questions of methodology, and what serves the understanding of the human being, especially the child.

When we observe the full seriousness of the situation in which the whole of humanity, in particular children, have fallen into in this twentieth century, then it should be a spur to us to work well together. And let us not forget that festive moment when Waldorf education began, when we began to speak of the "pedagogy of the present and immediate future," arising during the present cultural epoch when the consciousness soul of humanity is developing.

Let us in particular keep before us this thought which shall truly fill our hearts and minds: that bound up with the spiritual movement of the present day are also the spiritual powers that guide the universe. If we believe in these good spiritual powers, then they will be the inspirers of our lives and we shall really be enabled to teach. (Recorded by Herbert Hahn)

On 7 September, the public opening of the Waldorf School was celebrated in the city park of Stuttgart. On 9 September, the twelve teachers who were about to take on the work of the school gathered together with Rudolf Steiner. They recalled that festive moment at the beginning of the first lecture of THE FOUNDATIONS OF HUMAN EXPERIENCE, of the prayer and the inner lifting to those spiritual powers "by whose instruction and mandate each one of us must certainly work." It is important to continually recreate the relationship with the spirit of the time, with the language of folk or community spirits, and with one's own higher being or angel. These are the beings of the "Third Hierarchy," whom we can thank for the impulses in our will, our feelings, our thoughts, our new ideas and our certainty of heart. How does one create the relationship to the third hierarchy so that there is a new way of knowing how to relate to the heavenly world? How does one recall oneself?

In the evening before your meditation (prayer), ask the Angels, Archangels and Archai that they might help you in your work on the following day.

In the morning, following the meditation (prayer), may you know that you are related to the spirits of the third hierarchy. (Rudolf Steiner's advice was recorded by Caroline von Heydebrand — the word "prayer" is added here.) ❖

◆ From *The Problems of Our Time*, 12–14 September 1919, Berlin, Rudolf Steiner Press and Anthroposophic Press, 1943.

Unless we reach a stage at which we can see things so as to absorb the impulses which work into our physical world out of the spiritual, unless we realize that the human being, just as he or she is connected through the bodily organization with the animal, plant and mineral kingdoms, is also connected in his spiritual organization with the Angeloi, Archangeloi and Archai (Angeloi as the guardians of personal development, folk spirits as guardians of the development of peoples in defined spaces, spirits of time as guardians of development throughout the ages), unless we can understand these things from their spiritual foundations — we can advance no further. Everything depends on the human being having courage and force today to look into the spiritual world. We are at the beginning of a hard struggle, in which will be stirred up all the instincts springing from the one half–truth that economic reality is the only reality, that everything belonging to the soul and spirit is ideology; and from the other half–truth that the only reality is the psychic spiritual, all outside it is ideology, Maya. These contradictions will let loose in human nature such instincts that the spiritual conflict will blaze for long periods in forms of which people at present have no idea. We must grasp this and learn how we are to raise ourselves, in harmony with our time, to a view of the spiritual world as we conceive it. It is this which the times themselves ordain and demand; to this we must turn our attention. (pp. 66-67)

New soul–qualities and attitudes arose in humanity and we can really only understand what has entered human evolution if we turn our spiritual vision to the forces active within it and see, for instance, their effects in the revolution which occurred in the middle of the fifteenth century. Some time has passed since then, and we are now approaching the crisis due to what swept over civilized mankind at that point and has developed up to the present time, this critical moment when humanity's full consciousness must be brought to bear upon it.

We have reached a time when human beings must awake to the consciousness that, as a human being, she or he has a position within the earth's history, and outside of the human being are the three natural kingdoms, the animal, plant and mineral. (We shall speak later of how this awakening is to be achieved.) To speak of this fact expresses only a half–truth from the standpoint of our modern consciousness, the consciousness, that is, of the fifth post–Atlantean epoch. Before that epoch, people could still speak of the three kingdoms as outside of themselves, because their view of the kingdoms of nature was essentially different. In earlier times, people understood them as being spiritually controlled. Modern human beings have lost that; they must regain the consciousness in which they look at the three kingdoms, knowing that, as they are related downwards to them, so they are related upwards to the three kingdoms of Angeloi, Archangeloi and Archai. The half–truth becomes a whole truth when so completed, when we can look up to the realm of these three spiritual kingdoms. Our physical body has a relation to the three natural kingdoms, our soul–spiritual to what lives in the three hierarchies; and while we change on the one side our relation to the three kingdoms of nature, so also we alter our relation to the three kingdoms of hierarchies that stand above us. I want to draw your attention today to this important fact in human evolution. . .(pp. 16-18)

The important thing now is to seek afresh, from us outwards, the connection with the activity of these beings. Hitherto they have approached us; they have worked on us. Now we must work for ourselves on the soul–spiritual that is in us. The result of that work, what we unveil out of the spiritual world through spiritual investigation, will become something in our human soul that will restore the interest of the beings of the three higher hierarchies. They will be in the thoughts and feelings belonging to us, which we acquire out of the spiritual world. In this way we shall once again link our own being to that of the higher hierarchies.

So important is what is happening in our time that we must describe it as "a change in the attitude of the divine world to the human world." Until now divine beings have worked at perfecting the physical picture of humanity; human beings must now begin to work from their own soul–content, in order to find the way back to the higher hierarchies. The difficulty of our time is that human beings are so proud of their external picture of a body, which has now reached its completion, and develop thoughts independently of the picture, thoughts having no connection with the spiritual world. Our real task, thus made so much more difficult, is to seek this connection from out of us, through devotion to spiritual knowledge, sensitiveness to it, and a will obedient to it. (pp. 22-23)

Consciousness soul must develop more and more in such a way that the beings of the higher hierarchies no longer work into the human being, for that would darken man's consciousness — but that he may consciously raise himself to them. The full, clear, day consciousness of human beings is established when they work their way upward to the beings of the higher hierarchies. Spiritual science is the beginning of such work, for it has not sprung from any arbitrary choice or caprice, but from the recognition of this revolution in our time.

But the human being most consciously develops many other things as well. She has always had to live according to karma, the great law of destiny; but she has not always possessed knowledge of it. How amazing it was when, in Lessing's *EDUCATION OF THE HUMAN RACE*, the consciousness of repeated earth–lives sprang forth from the new spiritual revolution! We are at the beginning of a time of change between one human being and another. Human relations have changed even as the relationship between the human being and the beings of the three higher hierarchies has changed. The way in which human life was nurtured in the past does indeed extend into our own time; but we would fail in our duty to the present if we did not emphasize that new relations between human beings must now enter. It was of no import in earlier times, one could say, for the duty was not yet laid upon human beings to develop consciousness embracing previous earth–lives. In earlier times, human beings made contact with one another without the thought, "In you, O Man, there lives a Soul which existed in the spiritual world before birth and before that in another earth-life." (pp. 24-25).

The teacher of the future will need a fine feeling for what is developing in the growing child as a result of earlier earth-lives, and this comprehension will be the great achievement in the education of the future. A social attitude must be created, built up upon a spiritual relation to other human beings in the consciousness that when a fellow human being stands before us, we have to deal with a soul which has been through a previous incarnation. (p. 26). ❖

◆ Also from *THE PROBLEMS OF OUR TIME.*

There is a secret, intimately connected with the present stage of human evolution, which is not known today. In earlier times, before the middle of the fifteenth century, it was not necessary to take much notice of it, but today it must be reckoned with. This mystery of life is that man, constituted as he is today in body, soul and spirit, every night looks, to a certain extent, at the events of the coming day, but without always carrying that vision over into full day–consciousness. It is his "angel" who has that clear consciousness. But what is experienced at night in community with that being whom we call the angel is a pre-vision of the coming day. This is no subject for human curiosity, but a matter for practical life. Only when the feeling of this fact fills our inner being can we make the right decisions and bring right thoughts into the course of daily life. Let us assume that a man has something definite to do, say at noon. This that he has to do has already been arranged by his angel and himself during the preceding night, though the fact is not necessarily kept in consciousness and human curiosity has no part in it. People should be filled with the conviction that, during the day, they should realize in a fruitful way what they have arranged at night in cooperation with this angel being. (pp. 44-45)

If the feeling had permeated men that their doings in the day were in harmony with the decisions made with their angels in the preceding night, how different events would [be]! These things must be spoken of now, to point out how man must learn to regard this life between birth and death as a continuation of the life of the spirit and soul that was his before birth. It must be made known that man in the future should be able to experience throughout his whole life, the revelation of the divine in his own being, and that through all his life in the day, this vivid consciousness should persist as: "What I do from morning until evening I have discussed with my angel while I slept." (pp. 45-46) ❖

The Human Being and Society:

Towards a Social Working Together

Thinking/Knowing—Feeling/Speaking—Willing/Doing
Science—Art—Religion

◆ From *THREE STAGES IN THE AWAKENING OF THE HUMAN SOUL*, Prague, 28 April 1923. Published as *THE WAKING OF THE HUMAN SOUL AND THE FORMING OF DESTINY* by Steiner Book Centre, North Vancouver, BC, 1983.

Processes of combustion in the human being and in the animal are entirely different. When the flame of this organic process takes the horizontal direction, it annuls what comes from conscience, from the moral nature; these forces cannot find entry. The reason why the processes of combustion in the human being are permeated with the forces of conscience is that the flame of the will in man rises vertically from the earth. The child adapts itself to receive the in-pouring forces of conscience just as it adapts itself to the condition of physical equilibrium. The moral nature, nay even the religious impulse, stream into the human being together with the process of learning to walk. The forces that come into play when the child gives up crawling and begins to walk are lofty and sublime and when we follow them back through the darkness in which the child's consciousness is enveloped, we are led to an even higher kind of intercourse, namely with the beings we call the archai, the primal powers. Everything the human being has lived through in pre-earthly existence echoes on. And if we add a third phrase to the prayerful form, "For my thinking I am grateful to the angels, and for speech I thank the archangels," then it would be, "For my place within the sphere of physical and moral forces in earthly existence, I thank the archai, who have themselves received this power from even higher beings."

But the point of real importance is that, during sleep, we shall approach these three hierarchies of the angeloi, archangeloi and archai in a worthy way. This is what needs to be especially impressed upon modern humanity, for how we draw near the angeloi depends upon the quality and content of our thinking during waking life. How a human being draws near the archangeloi depends upon whether his or her powers of speech have been worthily used; how he or she draws near the archai depends upon whether he or she has made right use of the faculty of movement and moral will. . .

The forces that bring us near the angeloi during sleep are exactly commensurate with the idealism in our thinking. Similarly, powerlessness to take the steps leading to the angeloi is commensurate with the materialism in our thinking. It can be observed that human beings whose thinking during their waking life had no element of idealism in it, lack the forces which bring them near the angeloi and during sleep they fall to the ahrimanic elemental beings to whom their thinking must then find its way. Most people have not the slightest idea of how a child learns to think! The child's thinking — directly after it has first learned how to think — is full of spirituality. It is wonderful to see how until the time when materialism gets hold of them, children in sleep are borne on wings each to his angel, how they are united with their angels during sleep. And so we can say that it is only through idealism, through the spiritualizing of thoughts, that we can make our way during sleep to those worlds whence we came forth in order to acquire the power of thinking on the earth as human beings among human beings.

And now, speech. Idealism in feelings and sentiments is as essential for intercourse with the archangels during sleep as idealism in thinking is essential for intercourse with the angels. To be able, when speaking to others, to imbue the words with warmth, with kindly feeling, to find the way into the soul of another, nor to be indifferent to human beings but to enter into their concerns with real interest — that is the idealistic attitude which, when the astral body and Ego have passed over into sleep, will imbue speech with the element of music, of melody. This kind of feeling gives the astral body and ego — which also come into play in speech — the strength to draw near the archangels, whereas unsocial, egoistic sentiments dissipate those forces in the world of ahrimanic elementary beings. So that a man who has not used his power of speech worthily or imbued it with idealism really "dehumanizes" himself when he passes into sleep.

And again it is the same when our acts and deeds are philanthropic and performed in full consciousness. Then the human being is not only the being who lives in the flesh but in his innermost nature is a spiritual being. It is from this consciousness that respect for other human beings as spiritual beings is born. Out of such acts and deeds we acquire the power that brings us near the archai during sleep; whereas if we are incapable of such deeds, if we are conscious of ourselves only as beings of flesh, the forces are dispersed in the world of the ahrimanic elementary beings and we alienate ourselves from true humanity.

Thus the human being brings with him three gifts from pre–earthly existence. In a threefold way between sleeping and waking he links these gifts with what they are in their primal form. The individual remains unconscious, but ever and again draws near to the beings of the hierarchies. Just as here on earth there are three sources upon which we must draw in order to have intercourse with human beings — the source of thinking, of speech, and of action — so during sleep we have a threefold relationship with the spiritual world — with the angeloi, archangeloi, and archai. ❖

◆ The remarks were given by Rudolf Steiner at the opening celebration of the first Waldorf school on 7 September 1919. The German is printed at the end of *ALLEGMEINE MENSCHENKUNDE*, but is not included in the English translation, *STUDY OF MAN*, or in the more recent edition entitled *FOUNDATIONS OF HUMAN EXPERIENCE*.

This new school shall really be established for what is needed now and in the immediate future for the development of humanity. And in truth, all that ultimately flows from these concerns into the being of teaching and education forms a three–fold holy duty.

Of what importance ultimately is all self–feeling, knowing, and working in human society, if they cannot flow together in the holy obligation of teachers and educators in the service to society which they perform in working with the awakening, growing human child!

All that we can ultimately know about humanity and about the world will only become fruitful if we can pass it on in a living way to those who will form the social world when we are no longer present with our physical work.

All that we bring forward in an artistic way will reach its highest point only if we can let it flow into the greatest art, in which the materials are not lifeless clay and color but living people, as yet unfinished, whom we, in a certain way, should complete artistically and educationally.

And it is not finally a high, holy, religious duty, a godly-spiritual one, to care for the education of each human being who is born, who appears anew and reveals himself or herself? Is not this educational service a religious ritual in the highest sense of the word? Must not all our most holy human strivings, precisely those devoted to religious feeling, flow together in the altar service which we perform as we seek to further in the developing child, the divine spirit which reveals its presence in human beings!

Science becoming alive!
Art becoming alive!
Religion becoming alive!
That is education.
That is teaching.

◆ from *AWAKENING TO COMMUNITY* pp. 34–35.

The human being can orient himself rightly in the world only if the spirit within him finds the spirit outside him. The spirit that an older humanity found living in the world beyond death can be rightly laid hold upon by people living on the earth today only if they are irradiated by the Christ, who descended to earth from the same world whence rationality, intellectuality, and freedom made their way into the experience of incarnated human beings.

So we may say that anthroposophy begins in every case at the scientific level, calls right to the enlivening of its concepts, and ends in religious depending. It begins with what the head can grasp, takes on all the life and color of which words are capable, and ends in warmth that suffuses and reassures the heart, so that man's soul can at all times feel itself in the spirit, its true home. We must learn, on the anthroposophical path, to start with knowledge, then to life ourselves to the level of artistry, and to end in the warmth of religious feeling.

The present rejects this way of doing things, and that is why anthroposophy has enemies.

Receive the child in reverence,
Educate in love,
Let the child go forth in freedom.

◆ From *MANTRISCHE SPRÜCHE SEELENÜBUNGEN II*, 1903 –1925, (GA 268), Dornach: Rudolf Steiner Verlag, 1999, p. 276, Archive A0117, 1922.

Out of the seriousness of time
Must be born
The courage to act.

Give to the lessons, the education,
What the spirit gives you,
And you will free humanity
From the burden of materialism
That it bears.

To educate youth is
To foster the spirit in things,
To find tomorrow in today,
To cultivate the being of spirit in life on earth.

✦ From *Verses and Meditations*, London: Rudolf Steiner Press, 1979, p. 117, (GA263/1), November 1920.

The healthy social life is found
when in the mirror of each human soul
the whole community finds its reflection,
and when in the community
the virtue of each one is living.

✦ From *The Life, Nature, and Cultivation of Anthroposophy*, (GA 260a), London: Rudolf Steiner Press, 1989, p. 44, (1963) Please note that this was not a verse in original German.

When human beings honestly
seek the spiritual together,
they will also find the way
to each other from soul to soul.

✦ From *Verses and Meditations*, p. 85. Also from *Wahrspuchworte*, (GA 40), Dornach: Rudolf Steiner Verlag, 1998, p. 305, Archive 3975.

We of the present time
Need to give ear to the Spirit's morning call —
The call of Michael.
Spiritual Knowledge seeks
To open in the soul of man
True hearing of this morning call.

When in Danger

✦ From *MANTRISCHE SPRÜCHE SEELENÜBUNGEN II*, p. 190, Archive A-5345, undated.

You spirit of my life,
Be thou the goodness of heart
In my will,
Be thou the love of humanity
In my feeling,
Be thou the light of truth
In my thinking.

Prayer for Teachers and Educators

✦ From *CHILD'S CHANGING CONSCIOUSNESS*, (GA 306), 15-27 April 1923, Anthroposophic Press and Rudolf Steiner Press, (1988), Lecture 6, pp. 145-146.

Only such an attitude will lead to the realization that all education is, fundamentally, a self-education. Essentially, there is not education other than self-education, whatever the level may be. This is recognized in its full depth within anthroposophy, which has conscious knowledge through spiritual investigations of repeated Earth lives. Every education is self-education, and as teachers we can only provide the environment: for children's self-education. We have to provide the most favorable conditions where, through our agency, children can educate themselves according to their own destinies.

This is the attitude that teachers should have toward children, and such an attitude can be developed only through an ever-growing awareness of this fact. For people in general these may be many kinds of prayers. Over and above these there is a special prayer for the teachers:

Dear God,
Cause that I — inasmuch as my personal ambitions are concerned —
negate myself. And Christ make true in me the Pauline words, "Not I,
but the Christ in me."

This prayer, addressed to God in general and to Christ in particular, continues: ". . .*so that the Holy Spirit may hold sway in the teacher.*" This is the true Trinity.

If one can live in these thoughts while in close proximity to the students, then the hoped-for results of this education can become a social act at the same time. But other matters also come into play, and I can only touch on them. Just consider what, in the opinion of many people, would have to be done to improve today's social order. People expect better conditions through the implementation of external measures. You need only look at the dreadful experiments being carried out in Soviet Russia. There the happiness of the whole world is sought through the inauguration of external programs. It is believed that improvements in the social sphere depend on the creation of institutions. And yet, these are the least significant factors within social development. You can set up any institutions you like, be they monarchist or republican, democratic or socialist; the decisive factor will always be the kind of people who live and work under any of these systems. For those who spread a socializing influence, the two things that matter are a loving devotion toward what they are doing and an understanding interest in what the others are doing. ❖

Basic exercises given by Rudolf Steiner to those aspiring towards inner development.

◆ From the chapter entitled *"General Demands which Every Aspirant for Occult Development Must Put to Himself,"* GUIDANCE IN ESOTERIC TRAINING, Rudolf Steiner Press, London, (1998), pp. 13-19. (This was not included in the German original of this booklet.)

In what follows, the conditions which must be the basis of any occult development are set forth. Let no one imagine that he can make progress by any measures applied to the outer or the inner life unless he fulfills these conditions. All exercises in meditation, concentration, or exercises of other kinds, are valueless, indeed in a certain respect actually harmful, if life is not regulated in accordance with these conditions. No forces can actually be imparted to a human being; all that can be done is to bring to development the forces already within him. They do not develop of their own accord because outer and inner hindrances obstruct them. The outer hindrances are lessened by means of the following rules of life; the inner hindrances by the special instructions concerning meditation, concentration, and the like.

The first condition is the cultivation of absolutely clear thinking. For this purpose a man must rid himself of the will-o'the-wisps of thought, even if only for a very short time during the day — about five minutes (the longer, the better). He must become the ruler in his world of thought. He is not the ruler if external circumstances, occupation, some tradition or other, social relationships, even membership of a particular race, the daily round of life, certain activities and so forth, determine a thought and how he works it out. Therefore during this brief time, acting entirely out of his own free will, he must empty the soul of the ordinary, everyday course of thoughts and by his own initiative place one single thought at the center of his soul. The thought need not be a particularly striking or interesting one. Indeed it will be all the better for what has to be attained in an occult respect if a thoroughly uninteresting and insignificant thought is chosen. Thinking is then impelled to act out of its own energy, the essential thing here, whereas an interesting thought carries the thinking along with it. It is better if this exercise in thought control is undertaken with a pin rather than with Napoleon. The pupil says to himself, "Now I start from this thought, and through my own inner initiative, I associate with it everything that is pertinent to it." At the end of the period the thought should be just as colorful and living as it was at the beginning. This exercise is repeated day by day for at least a month; a new thought may be taken every day, or the same thought may be adhered to for several days. At the end of the exercise an endeavor is made to become fully conscious of that inner feeling of firmness and security which will soon be noticed by paying subtler attention to one's own soul; the exercise is then brought to a conclusion by focusing the thinking upon the head and the middle of the spine (brain and spinal cord), as if the feeling of security were being poured into this part of the body.

When this exercise has been practiced for, say, one month, a second requirement should be added. We try to think of some action that in the ordinary course of life we should certainly not have performed. Then we make it a duty to perform this action every day. It will therefore be good to choose an action that can be performed every day and will occupy as long a period of time as possible. Again it is better to begin with some insignificant action that we have to force ourselves to perform; for example, to water at a fixed time every day a flower we have bought. After a certain time a second, similar act should be added to the first — later, a third, and so on; as many as are compatible with the carrying out of all other duties. This exercise, also, should last for one month. But as far as possible during this second month, too, the first exercise should continue, although it is a less paramount duty than in the first month. Nevertheless it must not be left unheeded, for otherwise it will quickly be noticed that the fruits of the first month are lost and the slovenliness of uncontrolled thinking begins again. Care must be taken that once these fruits have been won, they are never again lost. If, through the second exercise, this initiative of action has been achieved, then, with subtle attentiveness, we become conscious of the feeling of an inner impulse of activity in the soul; we pour this feeling into the body, letting it stream down from the head to a point just about the heart.

In the third month, life should be centered on a new exercise — the development of certain equanimity towards the fluctuations of joy and sorrow, pleasure and pain — "heights of jubilation" and "depths of despair" should quite consciously be replaced by an equable mood. Care is taken that no pleasure shall carry us away, no sorrow plunge us into the depths, no experience lead to immoderate anger or vexation, no expectation give rise to anxiety or fear, no situation disconcert us, and so on. There need be no fear that such an exercise will make life arid and unproductive; rather it will quickly be noted that the experiences to which this exercise is applied are replaced by purer qualities of soul. Above all, if subtle attentiveness is maintained, an inner tranquility in the body will one day become noticeable; as in the two cases above, we pour this feeling into the body, letting it stream from the heart towards the hands, the feet and, finally, the head. This naturally cannot be done after each exercise, for here it is not a matter of one single exercise but of a sustained attentiveness to the inner life of the soul. Once every day, at least, this inner tranquility should be called up before the soul and then the exercise of pouring it out from the heart should proceed. A connection with the exercises of the first and second month is maintained, as in the second month with the exercise of the first month.

In the fourth month, as a new exercise, what is sometimes called a positive attitude to life should be cultivated. It consists in seeking always for the good, the praise—worthy, the beautiful and the like, in all beings, all experiences, and all things. This quality of soul is best characterized by a Persian legend concerning Christ Jesus. One day, as He waswalking with His disciples, they saw a dead dog lying by the roadside in a state of advanced decomposition. All the disciples turned away from the disgusting sight. Christ Jesus alone did not move but looked thoughtfully at the corpse and said: "What beautiful teeth the animal has!" Where the others had seen only the repulsive, the unpleasant, He looked for the beautiful. So must the esoteric pupil strive to seek for the positive in every phenomenon and in every being. He will soon notice that under the veil of something repugnant there is a hidden beauty, that even under the outer guise of a criminal there is a hidden good; that under the mask of a lunatic the divine soul is somehow concealed.

In a certain respect this exercise is connected with what is called "abstention from criticism." This is not to be understood in the sense of calling black white and white black. There is, however, a difference between a judgment which, proceeding merely from one's own personality, is colored with the element of personal sympathy or antipathy, and an attitude which enters lovingly into the alien phenomenon or being, always asking, "How has it come to be like this or to act like this?" Such an attitude will, by its very nature, be more set upon helping what is imperfect than upon simply finding fault and criticizing.

The objection that the very circumstances of their lives oblige many people to find fault and condemn is not valid here. For in such cases the circumstances are such that the person in question cannot go through a genuine occult training. There are indeed many circumstances in life that make occult schooling impossible, beyond a certain point. In such a case the person should not impatiently desire, in spite of everything, to make progress that is possible only under some conditions.

He who consciously turns his mind, for one month, to the positive aspect of all his experiences will gradually notice a feeling creeping into him as if his skin were becoming porous on all sides, and as if his soul were opening wide to all kinds of secret and delicate processes in his environment with hitherto entirely escaped his notice. The important point is to combat a very prevalent lack of attentiveness to these subtle things. If it has once been noticed that the feeling described expresses itself in the soul as a kind of bliss, endeavors should be made in thought to guide this feeling to the heart and, from there, to let it stream into the eyes, and thence out into the space in front of and around one—self. It will be noticed that an intimate relationship to this surrounding space is thereby acquired. A man grows out of and beyond himself, as it were. He learns to regard a part of his environment as something that belongs to him. A great deal of concentration is necessary for this exercise, and, above all, recognition of the fact that all tumultuous feelings, passions, and over—exuberant emotions have an absolutely destructive effect upon the mood indicated. The exercises of the first months are repeated, as with the earlier months.

In the fifth month, efforts should be made to develop the feeling of confronting every new experience with complete open-mindedness. The esoteric pupil must break entirely with the attitude that, in the face of something just heard or seen, exclaims: "I never heard that, or I never saw that, before. I don't believe it — it is an illusion." At every moment he must be ready to encounter and accept absolutely new experiences. What he has hitherto recognized as being in accordance with natural law, or what he has regarded as possible, should present no obstacle to the acceptance of a new truth. Although radically expressed, it is absolutely correct that if anyone were to come to the esoteric pupil and say, "Since last night the steeple of such and such a church has been tilted right over," the esoterist should leave a loophole open for the contingency of his becoming convinced that his previous knowledge of natural law could somehow be augmented by such an apparently unprecedented fact. If he turns his attention, in the fifth month, to developing this attitude of mind, he will notice creeping into his soul a feeling as if something were becoming alive, astir, in the space referred to in connection with the exercise for the fourth month. This feeling is exceedingly delicate and subtle. Efforts must be made to be attentive to this delicate vibration in the environment and to let it stream, as it were, through all the five senses, especially through the eyes, the ears and through the skin, in so far as the latter contains the sense of warmth. At this stage of esoteric development, less attention is paid to the impressions made by these stimuli on the other senses of taste, smell and touch. At this stage it is still not possible to distinguish the numerous bad influences that intermingle with the good influences in this sphere; the pupil therefore leaves this for a later stage.

In the sixth month, endeavors should be made to repeat all the five exercises again, systematically and in regular alternation. In this way a beautiful equilibrium of soul will gradually develop. It will be noticed, especially, that previous dissatisfactions with certain phenomena and beings in the world completely disappear. A mood reconciling all experiences takes possession of the soul, a mood that is by no means one of indifference but, on the contrary, enables one for the first time to work in the world for its genuine progress and improvement. One comes to a tranquil understanding of things that were formerly quite closed to the soul. The very movements and gestures of a person change under the influence of such exercises, and if, one day, he can actually observe that the character of his handwriting has altered, then he may say to himself that he is just about to reach a first rung on the upward path.

Once again, two things must be stressed: First, the six exercises described paralyze the harmful influence other occult exercises can have, so that only what is beneficial remains. Secondly, these exercises alone ensure that efforts in meditation and concentration will have a positive result. The esotericist must not rest content with fulfilling, however conscientiously, the demands of conventional morality, for that kind of morality can be extremely egotistical, if a man says: I will be good in order that I may be thought good. The esotericist does not do what is good because he wants to be thought good, but because little by little he recognizes that the good alone brings evolution forward, and that evil, stupidity and ugliness place hindrances along its path. ❖

✦ From *Guidance in Esoteric Training*, (GA 245), Rudolf Steiner Press, 1998, pp. 24–27.

The pupil must pay careful attention to certain activities in the life of soul that in the ordinary way are carried on carelessly and inattentively. There are eight such activities.

It is naturally best to undertake only one exercise at a time, throughout a week or a fortnight, for example, then the second, and so on, then beginning over again. Meanwhile it is best for the eighth exercise to be carried out every day. True self-knowledge is then gradually achieved and any progress made is perceived. Then later on, beginning with Saturday, one exercise lasting for about five minutes may perhaps be added daily to the eighth so that the relevant exercise will fall on the same day. Thus: Saturday — thoughts; Sunday — resolves; Monday — talking; Tuesday — actions; Wednesday — behavior, and so on.

Saturday

To pay attention to one's ideas.

To think only significant thoughts. To learn, little by little, to separate in one's thoughts the essential from the non-essential, the eternal from the transitionary, truth from mere opinion.

In listening to the talk of one's fellow men, to try and become quite still inwardly, forgetting all assent and still more, all unfavorable judgments (criticism, rejection), even in one's thoughts and feelings.

This may be called: "RIGHT OPINION."

Sunday

To determine even the most insignificant matter only after fully reasoned deliberation. All unthinking behavior, all meaningless actions, should be kept far away from the soul. One should always have well weighed reasons for everything. And one should definitely abstain from doing anything for which there is no significant reason.

Once one is convinced of the rightness of a decision, one must hold fast to it, with inner steadfastness and without relying on sympathy or antipathy.

This may be called: "RIGHT JUDGMENT,"
having been formed independently of sympathies and antipathies.

Monday

Talking. Only what has sense and meaning should come from the lips of one striving for higher development. All talking for the sake of talking — to kill time — is in this sense harmful.

The usual kind of conversation, a disjointed medley of remarks, should be avoided. This does not mean shutting oneself off from intercourse with one's fellows; it is precisely then that talk should gradually be led to significance. One adopts a thoughtful attitude to every speech and answer, taking all aspects into account. Never talk without cause — be gladly silent. One tries not to talk too much or too little. First listen quietly; then reflect on what has been said.

This exercise may be called: "RIGHT WORD."

Tuesday

External Actions. These should not be disturbing for our fellowman. Where an occasion calls for action out of one's inner being, deliberate carefully how one can best meet the occasion — for the good of the whole, the lasting happiness of man, the eternal. Where one does things of one's own accord, out of one's own initiative, consider most thoroughly beforehand the effect of one's actions.

This is called: "RIGHT DEED."

Wednesday

The ordering of life. To live in accordance with nature and spirit. Not to be swamped by the external trivialities of life. To avoid all that brings unrest and haste into life. To hurry over nothing, but also not to be indolent. To look on life as a means for working towards higher development and to behave accordingly.

One speaks in this connection of: "RIGHT STANDPOINT."

Thursday

Human endeavor. One should take care to do nothing that lies beyond one's powers — but also to leave nothing undone which lies within them.

To look beyond the everyday, the momentary, and to set oneself aims and ideals connected with the highest duties of a human being. For instance, in the sense of the prescribed exercises, to try to develop oneself so that afterwards, one may be able all the more to help and advise one's fellowmen — though perhaps not in the immediate future.

This can be summed up as:
"TO LET ALL THE FOREGOING EXERCISES BECOME A HABIT."

Friday

The endeavor to learn as much as possible from life.

Nothing goes by us without giving us a chance to gain experiences that are useful for life. If one has done something wrongly or imperfectly, that becomes a motive for doing it rightly or more perfectly later on.

If one sees others doing something, one observes them with the same end in view (yet not coldly or heartlessly). And one does nothing without looking back to past experiences that can be of assistance in one's decisions and achievements.

One can learn from everyone — even from children if one is attentive.

This exercise is called: "RIGHT MEMORY."
Remembering what has been learned from experiences.

Summary

To turn one's gaze inward from time to time, even if only for five minutes daily at the same time. In doing so one should sink down into oneself, carefully take counsel with oneself, test and form one's principles of life, run through in thought one's knowledge — or lack of it — weigh up one's duties, think over the contents and true purpose of life, feel genuinely pained by one's own errors and imperfections. In a word — labor to discover the essential, the enduring and earnestly aim at goals in accord with it, for instance, virtues to be acquired. (Not to fall into the mistake of thinking that one has done something well, but to strive ever further towards the highest standards.)

This exercise is called: "RIGHT EXAMINATION."

The Twelve Monthly Virtues

✦ From *GUIDANCE IN ESOTERIC TRAINING*, p. 28.
Monthly virtues to be meditated upon and observed in one's life.

APRIL ◇	Devotion ◇	becomes the power of sacrifice
MAY ◇	Balance ◇	becomes progress
JUNE ◇	Perseverance ◇	becomes faithfulness
JULY ◇	Unselfishness ◇	becomes catharsis
AUGUST ◇	Compassion ◇	becomes freedom
SEPTEMBER ◇	Courtesy ◇	becomes steadiness of feeling
OCTOBER ◇	Contentment ◇	becomes self- composure
NOVEMBER ◇	Patience ◇	becomes understanding
DECEMBER ◇	Control of speech ◇	becomes a feeling for the truth and thinking.. (minding one's tongue)
JANUARY ◇	Courage ◇	becomes the power of redemption
FEBRUARY ◇	Discretion ◇	becomes the power of meditation
MARCH ◇	Magnanimity ◇	becomes love

These exercises should always be begun on the 21st of the preceding month.
For example, April's practice should be from 21 March to 20 April.

◆ From the lecture *"The Nature of Prayer,"* 17 February 1910, Berlin in *METAMORPHOSIS OF THE SOUL, PATHS OF EXPERIENCE, VOLUME II*, (GA 58), Rudolf Steiner Press, London, (1983), p. 45.

Whatever the next hour or day may bring, I cannot change it by fear and anxiety, for it is not yet known. I will therefore wait for it with complete inward restfulness, perfect tranquility of mind.

Anyone who can meet the future in this calm, relaxed way, without impairing his active strength and energy, will be able to develop the powers of his soul freely and intensively. It is as if hindrance after hindrance falls away, as the soul comes to be more and more pervaded by this feeling of humbleness toward approaching events.

This feeling of submission springs from that mode of prayer, directed towards the future and the wisdom-filled course of events therein. To give ourselves over to this divine wisdom means that we call up again and again the thoughts, feelings and impulses that go with a recognition that what will come must come and that in one direction or another it must have good effects.❖

Initiative

◆ From *KARMIC RELATIONSHIPS, VOLUME III*, (GA 237), Dornach, 4 August 1924, Anthroposophic Pub. Company, London, (1957).

From somewhere, out of the depths of my inner being, there will emerge the necessity for me to find inner initiative in life, initiative of soul which will enable me to undertake something or to make some judgment or decision out of my own inmost being.

Be a person of initiative, and beware, lest through hindrances of your own body, or hindrances that otherwise come in your way, you fail to find the center of your being, the source of your initiative. Observe that in your life all joy and sorrow, all happiness and pain, will depend on the finding or not finding of your own individual initiative. This should stand written, as though in golden letters, constantly before the soul of the anthroposophist. Initiative lies in his karma, and much of what meets him in his life will depend on the extent to which he can become willingly, actively conscious of it. ❖

✦ From *VERSES AND MEDITATIONS*, p. 161.
Rudolf Steiner gave this verse to a worker at the Waldorf-Astoria cigarette factory
who had grown deaf. The verse was conveyed by Herbert Hahn.

In the beginning was Christ
And Christ was with the Gods,
And a God was Christ,
Deep in each human soul
Being of Christ indwells.
In my soul too He dwells,
And He will lead me
To the true meaning of my life.

Further Verses for Self–Education

✦ *VERSES AND MEDITATIONS*, p. 155.

Dwelling in silence on the beauties of life
Gives the soul strength of Feeling.

Thinking clearly on the truths of existence
Brings to the Spirit the light of Will.

✦ From *WAHRSPUCHWORTE*, p. 255, 15 May 1906, Archive A-0183.

Whoever strives toward Spirit
May have enduring hope
That when he is in need,
He will not be without the guidance of Spirit.

✦ From *WAHRSPUCHWORTE*, p. 247, Archive 3989, ca. 1904.

Seek the Light of the Path!
But you will seek in vain,
If you do not yourself become Light.

◆ *SOURCES UNKNOWN.*

The human being will unfold
By kindling in the soul fire of love
The shining wisdom of Spirit.

◆ From *TRUTH–WROUGHT–WORDS*, p. 57.

The soul's questings are quickening
The will's deeds are waxing
And life's fruits grow ripe

I feel my destiny,
My destiny finds me.
I feel my star,
My star finds me.
I feel my goals,
My goals find.

My soul and the World are but one.

Life becomes brighter about me,
Life becomes harder for me,
Life becomes richer within me.

◆ From *WAHRSPUCHWORTE*, p. 160; 9 July 1924, (GA 279); and 1914, (GA 277a.)

Strive for peace,
Live in peace,
Love peace.

◆ From *WAHRSPUCHWORTE*, p. 256, 1906/1907, Archive A-0126.

The meaning of the world is realized
In the human being's deeds that are
Illuminated by wisdom and warmed by love.

✦ Retranslated from *WAHRSPUCHWORTE,* p. 213.

Genuine self-knowledge will only come to the human being
When he or she develops loving interest in others;
Genuine world-knowledge will only come to the human being
When he or she seeks to understand his or her own nature.

✦ *SOURCES UNKNOWN.*

If I strive toward
Clarity of thought,
Depth of feeling,
Calmness of will.
Then I may hope
To find my way
On life's paths,
Before human hearts,
And in the realm of duty.

✦ Retranslated from *VERSES AND MEDITATIONS,* p. 171.

For clarity
Comes from light of spirit,
And depth
Preserves warmth of spirit,
Calm strengthens vitality.
And when I strive for all of this
Out of trust in God
It will guide me on human pathways
By right and confident life steps.

◆ *SOURCES UNKNOWN.*

May the protective and blessed ray of God
Fill my growing soul
That it may take hold
Of universal strengthening powers.
My soul vows to awaken in itself
The power of love in a living way.
And to see God's strength
In its life path,
And to work in God's way
With all that it has.

◆ From *WAHRSPUCHWORTE,* p. 252, 2 February 1906, Archive 3992.

Joys are gifts of destiny,
Which prove their worth in the present,
But sorrows are sources of knowledge,
Whose meaning will be shown in the future.

◆ From *WAHRSPUCHWORTE,* p. 334, 1919, Archive 5374.

The sun gives light to the plants
For the sun loves the plants
In the same way a human being gives
Light of the soul to others
If he loves them.

✦ *FROM PRAYERS FOR PARENTS AND CHILDREN*, London: Rudolf Steiner Press, 1995, p. 19.

The Light of the Sun
Brightens all space
When dark night is past.
The life of the soul
Now is awakened
From restful sleep.
O thou my soul,
Give thanks to the Light.
In it shines forth
The power of God.
O thou, my soul,
Be strong for deeds.

At the Ringing of the Bells

✦ From *TRUTH-WROUGHT-WORDS*, p. 13.

To wonder at beauty,
Stand guard over truth,
Look up to the noble,
Decide for the good:
Leads us on our journey
To goals for our life,
To right in our doing,
To peace in our feeling,
To light in our thought,
And teaches us trust
In the guidance of God,
In all that there is
In the world-wide All,
In the soul's deep soil.

Evenings

✦ From *TRUTH-WROUGHT-WORDS*, p. 81.

From my head to my feet
I'm the picture of God.
From my heart into my hands,
I feel the God's living breath.
When I speak with my mouth,
I follow God's own will.
When I gaze on God
In the whole world-all
In father and mother,
In all dear people,
In beast and flower,
In tree and stone,
No fear can come near,
Only love,
For all that's around me here.

Mornings

✦ From *PRAYERS FOR PARENTS AND CHILDREN*, p. 11.

When I see the sun,
I think God's spirit,
When I use my hand,
God's soul lives in me.
And when I see a human being,
God's soul lives in him.
And so, too, God's soul
Lives in father, in mother,
In animal and flower,
In tree and stone.
Fear can never reach me
When I thank God's spirit,
When I live in God's soul,
When I walk with God's will.

✦ From *WAHRSPUCHWORTE*, p. 136.

Seek the truly practical material life
but seek it in such a way
that it does not numb you
to the spirit that works within it.
Seek the spirit,
but not out of spiritual lust
or spiritual egoism;
seek it rather
because you wish to become selfless in the practical life
wanting to turn to the material world.

Turn to the ancient principle:
"Spirit is never without matter, matter never without spirit!"

✦ From *THE SPIRIT OF THE WALDORF SCHOOL*, (GA 297), Hudson, NY:
Anthroposophic Press, 1995, p. 98, 24 September 1919.

In such a way say to yourselves:
We will do everything material in the light of the spirit,
and we will seek the light of the spirit in such a way
that it enkindles warmth in us for our practical deeds.

• *But Mary took all these words into her heart.* (Gospel of Luke)

• *Meditation means to warm a thought in the heart.*

• *Knowledge if the Light and Love is the Light's warmth.* (R.S.)

• *Anthroposophical ideas are vessels fashioned by love,*
  And Man's being is spiritually summoned by the spiritual world
  To partake of their content.

✦ From *OUTLINE OF ESOTERIC SCIENCE,* Anthroposophic Press, 1997, p. 321.

To come to clarity on this point, we must realize that human thinking, if it gets a strong inner grip on itself, can comprehend much more than we usually imagine it can. There is an inner entity inherent in thought itself that already has connections to the supersensible world. The soul is usually not aware of these connections because it is in the habit of developing its thinking abilities only by applying them to the sensory world.

✦ From *THE FOUNDATIONS OF HUMAN EXPERIENCE,* Third Lecture,
Anthroposophic Press, 1996, p. 68.

Above these two activities, the comprehension through the intellect of what is dead and the comprehension through the will of what is living, is something that only human beings and no other earthly beings carry within themselves from birth until death. That is pure thinking, thinking unrelated to external nature, but related to the supersensible in human beings, to what makes human beings independent beings and to something that is above the sub-dead and super-living. If we wish to speak of human freedom, then we must respect this aspect of autonomy in human beings; we must look at the pure sense-free thinking in which the will always lives.

✦ From *BALANCE IN TEACHING*, Mercury Press, 1982, pp. 41-42.

The studies that a spiritual scientific pedagogy undertakes have as their aim a more intimate knowledge of the human being. But if you then think about these things in meditation you cannot help affecting their continued action within yourself. If, for instance, you eat a piece of bread, you are first concerned with a conscious process; but what then takes place, when the bread passes through the complicated process of digestion, is something which you can affect but little; yet this process takes its course and your general life is closely bound up with it. Now, if you study the human being as we have done, you experience it at first consciously; but if afterwards you meditate upon it, an inner spiritual-psychic process of digestion takes place within you, and this is what makes you an educator or teacher, just as a healthy metabolic process makes an active human being out of you, so this meditative digestion of a true knowledge of man makes you into an educator. It is simply that you confront the child as an educator in an entirely different manner if you have lived through what results from a genuine, spiritual-scientific knowledge of the human being. In fact, that which makes us educators grows out of the meditative work of acquiring such knowledge. And observations such as we have made active today the inner soul-life if we keep reawakening them within ourselves and devote even five minutes a day to them. We become so fertile in thought and feeling that what we have to give fairly bubbles forth from us. Meditate in the evening upon such knowledge of man, and in the morning there springs to your mind: yes, I must undertake this or that with Jack Miller; or that girl lacks this or that, and so forth. In short, you know what you should do in each specific case.

It is important in human life to bring about this sort of cooperation between the inner and the outer life. This does not even require very much time. Once you have mastered such things inwardly you can acquire in three seconds what you will do for a whole day in the language of instruction, applying it to education. Time loses its significance when it is a case of calling the supersensible to life. ❖

✦ From AN OUTLINE OF ESOTERIC SCIENCE, pp. 289–295. Anthroposophic Press, 1997.

It is only possible to rise to a state of supersensible consciousness from ordinary waking consciousness, the state the soul lives in prior to its ascent. Training provides the soul with methods that will lead it out of the ordinary waking state. Among the first methods provided by the training we are discussing here are some that can still be described as functions of ordinary waking consciousness. The most important of these consist of silent activities of the soul. The soul is meant to devote itself to certain specific mental images that have the intrinsic power to awaken certain hidden faculties in the human soul. Such mental images are different from those of our daily waking life, whose purpose is to depict outer things — the more truly they do this, the truer they themselves are, and it is part of their essential nature to be "true" in this sense. This is not the purpose of the mental images the soul concentrates on when its goal is spiritual training. These images are not structured so as to reproduce anything external, but to have an awakening effect on the soul. The best thought pictures for this purpose are symbolic ones, but others can be used also. The content of these mental images is not the point; the point is that the soul devotes all its energies to having nothing in its consciousness other than the mental image in question.

In our everyday soul life, the soul's energies are divided among many different things and our mental images shift rapidly. In spiritual training, however, the point is to concentrate the soul's entire activity on a single mental image that is freely chosen as a focus for consciousness. For this reason, symbolic images are better than ones that represent outer objects or processes and have a point of contact with the outer world, since these do not force the soul to rely on itself to the same extent as it does with symbols that it creates out of its own energy. It is not important what is imagined, but only that the process of visualizing the image frees the soul from dependence on anything physical.

By calling to mind the concept of memory, we can begin to grasp what it means to immerse ourselves in visualized image. For example, if we look at a tree and then turn away from it so that we can no longer see it, we can reawaken the mental image of the tree out of our memory. The mental image we have of a tree when it is not actually present before our eyes is the memory of a tree. Now let us imagine that we retain this memory in our soul; we allow the soul to rest on this memory image and attempt to exclude all other images. Then the soul is immersed in the memory image of the tree. But although the soul is immersed in a mental image, this image is a copy of something perceived by our senses. However, if we attempt the same thing with an image that we insert into our consciousness through an act of free will, we will gradually be able to achieve the necessary effect.

We will illustrate this with a single example of contemplating or meditating on a symbolic mental image. First, this mental image must be built up in the soul. I can do this as follows: I imagine a plant taking root in the ground, sprouting one leaf after another, and continuing to develop up to the point of flowering. Then I imagine a human being alongside this plant. In my soul, I bring to life the thought that this human being has qualities and abilities that can be called more perfect than those of the plant. I think about how human beings are able to move around in response to their feelings and intentions, while plants are attached to the ground. But then I also notice that although human beings are certainly more perfect than plants, they also have characteristics that we cannot perceive in plants, characteristics whose absence can actually make plants seem more perfect than humans. Human beings are filled with desires and passions that their actions obey, and certain errors result from these drives and passions. In contrast, I see how plants obey the pure laws of growth as they develop one leaf after another and open their flowers without passion to the chaste rays of the Sun. I can say that human beings have an advantage over plants with regard to a certain type of perfection, but that the price they have paid for this perfection is to allow urges, desires, and passions to enter their nature alongside the forces of the plants that seem so pure to me.

Next I visualize the green sap flowing through the plant and imagine this as an expression of the pure, passionless laws of growth. Then I visualize the red blood flowing through human arteries and imagine it as an expression of urges, desires, and passions. I allow all this to arise in my soul as a vivid thought. Then I think about how human beings are capable of development, how they can use higher soul faculties to cleanse and purify their urges and passions. I think about how this destroys a baser element in these urges and passions, which are then reborn on a higher level. The blood may then be imagined as the expression of these cleansed and purified urges and passions. For example, in the spirit I see a rose and say: In the red sap of the rose blossom I see the color of the plants green sap transformed into red, and the red rose, like the green leaf, obeys the pure, passionless laws of growth. Let the red of the rose symbolize the blood that is an expression of purified urges and passions. They have been stripped of their baser element and are now similar in purity to the forces that are active in the red rose.

I now try not only to assimilate these thoughts with my intellect, but also to bring them to life in my feeling. I can have a blissful sensation when I imagine the growing plant's purity and absence of passion; I can generate a feeling in myself for the price human beings must pay for greater perfection by acquiring urges and desires. This can transform my earlier bliss into a serious feeling. Next, a feeling of liberating happiness can stir in me as I devote myself to the thought of the red blood that can become the vehicle of inwardly pure experiences, just like the red sap of the rose blossom.

It is important not to unfeelingly confront the thoughts that serve to build up a symbolic mental image such as this. After having basked in these thoughts and feelings, we transform them into this symbolic image: We imagine a black cross. Let this be the symbol of the baser element that has been eliminated from our urges and passions. We imagine seven radiant red roses arranged in a circle where the two beams of the cross intersect. Let these be the symbol of the blood that is an expression of cleansed, purified passions and urges.[1] This symbolic image must now be called up before our mind's eye in the way described earlier with regard to a memory image. A symbolic mental image such as this has the power to awaken our souls when we inwardly immerse ourselves in it and devote ourselves to it. We must try to exclude all other mental images while we are immersed in this one. We must allow only this symbol to linger before our mind's eye in the spirit, and it must be as vivid as possible.

It is not without significance that this symbol was not immediately proffered as a soul-awakening image, but was first built up by means of specific ideas about plants and human beings, because the effectiveness of a symbol like this depends on its being put together in this way before it is used for meditation. If we imagine it, without first having gone through this buildup in our own souls, the symbol remains cold and is much less effective than if it has received its soul–illuminating power through this preparation. During meditation, however, we should not summon up all of these preparatory thoughts, but should only allow the image to linger vividly before us in the spirit while permitting the feeling we had as a result of these preparatory thoughts to resonate. In this way, the symbol becomes a token of this experience of feeling, and its effectiveness is due to the fact that the soul dwells on this experience. The longer we can dwell on it without a different and disruptive image intervening, the more effective the whole process will be. However, outside of the time we set aside for actual meditation, it is a good idea to frequently repeat the process of building up the image through thoughts and feelings of the type described above, so that the feeling does not fade away. The more patience we have in renewing it, the more significant the image becomes for our souls. (Additional examples of methods of meditation are explained in my book, *HOW TO KNOW HIGHER WORLDS*.[2] Described there are meditations on becoming and dying in plants, the creative forces lying dormant in seeds, the forms of crystals, and so on, which are especially effective. The intent here was to use a single example to demonstrate the nature of meditation.)

A symbol such as the one described here is not a copy of any outer thing or being that nature has produced, but this very fact gives it the power to awaken certain faculties that are strictly soul–like in character. However, an objection could be raised to this. Someone might say, "It is true that the symbol as a whole is not present in nature, but all of its details have been borrowed from nature: the black color, the roses, and so on. All these things are perceived by the senses." Anyone who is bothered by this objection should consider the fact that the process of reproducing the sense perceptions is not what leads to awakening our higher soul faculties, but that this is brought about solely through how these details are combined, and the combination itself does not depict anything that is present in the world of the senses. ❖

The Influence of the Christ–Impulse
in the Course of Human History

✦ On 13 March 1911 in Berlin, in the lecture series entitled BACKGROUND TO THE GOSPEL OF ST. MARK, [(GA 124), Rudolf Steiner Press, London, 1985, p.146,] Rudolf Steiner portrayed how the "Sun stream of the Christ Impulse" determines the direction of human development. A preparation was made for Golgotha through the Jahve culture for about six hundred years. Then for about six hundred years Christianity lived into world history. Then Arabic thought burned its way into Europe as an accompanying stream. This continues today as scientific thought. Kepler and Copernicus are unthinkable without Arabism. Then, in the Renaissance culture, the stream of the Greek times returned. Today, again after six hundred years, a new accompanying stream enters in. It is necessary that we have an exact understanding of this influx and "Christianize" it. (von Kügelen)

Regarding this, Rudolf Steiner says the following:

Now we can ask ourselves: Which stream will enter directly into the culture in the future? That is the Christ-stream. It flows forward in a straight line. And what accompanying stream do we see indicated? First of all, we have the Arabic stream, which flowed in as a main stream and then had a quiet period and found new expression in the Renaissance culture. Now we have a renewed inflow from the Buddha stream. Those who would like to take these facts up in the right way will now say: We must therefore take up those elements out of the Buddha stream that, until now, were not contained in our western culture. Then we see that certain elements of the Buddha stream are flowing into the spiritual development of the West, such as the ideas of reincarnation and karma. These flow in now. However, we must sternly write something else in the soul: All these accompanying streams can give us no information about the central core of our world-view, our spiritual science. Buddhism or other pre-Christian oriental views that extend themselves into our time as a renewed world-view cannot be asked about the essence of the Christ. That would be like the European Christians asking the Arabs who came to Spain about the being of Christ. At that time the people of Europe understood that ideas about the Christ could not come to them from the Arabs, that they had nothing to say about the Christ. This needs to be clear to us, too, that the accompanying stream of Arabism can fructify us through entirely different elements, through the materialism of natural science, but in no way through information about the central mystery of the Christ.

in the Course of Human History

In exactly the same way we must place ourselves in relationship to each stream, which today flows towards us as an accompanying wave, like the renewal of an old wave which brings an understanding of reincarnation and karma. But is not possible for it to bring an understanding of the Christ impulse. For it to do so would be just as absurd as if the Arabs wanted to bring the correct Christ ideas to the Europeans. They were able to bring many ideas of false Messiahs to the Europeans, such as Sabbatai Zevi. Such things will happen again in new ways. The development of human beings can only go forward if people have strength enough to see through these things. And we must always look through these things with more and more clarity and penetration. It will therefore come about that this spiritual science with its central idea of the Christ, which was founded through European Rosicrucianism, will, despite all obstacles and all outer temptations, enter the minds of human beings. How the central idea of the Christ must be drawn into the minds of mankind, how the Christ is woven into the total evolution not only of mankind but of the cosmos, that you can take from my book, AN OUTLINE OF ESOTERIC SCIENCE. There is described the continually evolving way. All those who hear of this evolving spiritual science will have the possibility to understand words such as these from the Gospel of Mark:

"There will arise false Christs and false Prophets. . .When in time someone says to you: See here is Christ! See, there he is! Do not believe him."

Next to this stream, however, there stands another even further along, which believes itself better able to instruct about the nature of the Christ than can the western Rosicrucian spiritual science. From there will come all kinds of ideas and teachings from the views arising from the accompanying stream of oriental Buddhism. But it would be a sign of the greatest weakness for European souls if these European souls were not able to seize the thought: In the direct pursuit of the Christ idea the Mercury or Buddha stream brings as little light as the Arabic stream was able to bring to the pursuit of the Christ idea. This is not brought forward here out of a belief based on dogma or fantasy but rather out of the objective direction of world evolution. ❖

✦ From *DER TOD ALS LEBENSWANDLUNG*, (GA 182), 1917/18.
(No published English translation found.)

Y ou see, what I have just clarified occurs over and over again without end. All of you, as you sit here, are constantly in communication with the dead. People don't realize this in their ordinary lives because it takes place in the subconscious. The clairvoyant subconscious is not playing tricks; rather it merely elevates to consciousness what is present in the spiritual world. All of you are constantly in communication with the dead.

This realm of the hierarchies is what, on the other side, gives us the full intensity of our experience of the I between death and a new birth. Through the first two realms, we experience the other; we experience ourselves through the hierarchies. The human being as spiritual being experiences himself inside the hierarchies on the other side as a child of the hierarchies. He knows he is connected to the other human souls, as I have described it, but at the same time he also knows that he is a child of the hierarchies. In the same way that he feels himself to be the confluence of the outer natural powers of the surrounding cosmos — if indeed he sees himself in the cosmos — on the other side he feels himself to be organized as a spiritual being out of the collaboration of the various hierarchies.

As here our I is embedded in our physical body so that it is an extract of our outer nature, so is on the other side our spirituality embedded in the hierarchies — as an extract of the hierarchies. In other words, over there we are clothed in our spirituality in the way that here we clothe ourselves in our physical body when we pass over the threshold of birth.

It would be a giant step in the evolution of humanity if, for the part of earth life that humanity must still live through, human beings here would develop the following consciousness: In their feeling and willing lives they are united with the dead! Death can only rob us of the physical sight and the thoughts of the dead. But we cannot feel anything without the presence of the dead in our feeling space, and we cannot will anything without the presence of the dead in that sphere.

The greatest illusion that humanity of the future can have would be to believe that what it has developed as its social life here on earth with its will and feeling happened only through earthly arrangements. It cannot happen only through earthly arrangements because the dead indeed work together with us in our feeling and willing.

Now here is the point — how will it be possible to develop, within the impulses of modern times, consciousness of this kind of working together with the spiritual world? The evolution of Mankind works in such a way that, with ordinary consciousness here in the physical body, human beings actually distance themselves more and more from the spiritual world. Now in order for man as a physical being to find the right approach to the spiritual world during his earth evolution, the mystery of Golgotha occurred.

This mystery of Golgotha is not only a unique event and as such the greatest event in earth evolution, but it is an ongoing event, an ongoing impulse. And humanity must take action to allow this impulse to continue to work in the right way.

Today most of us believe that when the human being crosses the threshold of death, his or her activity with respect to the physical world stops. It does not stop. Ongoing, lively communication occurs between the so–called dead and the so–called living. We can even say that those who have passed over the threshold of death have not stopped being here, our eyes have stopped seeing them, but they are here. Our thoughts, our feelings, our will impulses are connected to them. The word of the Gospel also goes for the dead: "Look not for the realm of the spirit outside of yourselves, for it is among you."

One should not search for the dead randomly in the outside world, rather one should become conscious that they are always here. All historical, social, ethical life proceeds through the working together of the so-called living with the so-called dead. And the human being may experience a special strengthening of his being if he permeates himself more and more, not only with consciousness that comes with a secure hold in the physical world, but also with the consciousness that comes from saying to oneself with the right inner sense of the beloved dead: the dead are right here among us. This as well belongs to a right knowledge and right recognition of the spiritual world that is put together out of different pieces. One can say, "We know about the spiritual world in the right way if the way we think and speak about it comes itself out of this spiritual world."

The saying, "The dead are with us," is itself a strengthening of the spiritual world. And only the spiritual world can call forth in us a true consciousness that the dead are among us. ❖

✦ From *TRUTH-WROUGHT-WORDS*, p. 93.

Into spirit pastures I will send
The faithful love which here we found
That we might be united soul with soul.
So may you find my thinking ever loving
When from the spirit's light-filled lands
You, searching, turn your gaze of soul
To see what here in me you seek.

✦ Also from *TRUTH-WROUGHT-WORDS*.

The love of my soul
Strives to you,
My love's sensing
streams to you,
May they bear you aloft,
May they uphold you there,
In the heights of hope,
In the spheres of love.

✦ *SOURCES UNKNOWN.*

Feel how our loving gaze
Is lifted to the heights
That have called you away for other tasks.
Offer the friends left behind
Your strength from out of spiritual lands.

✦ *SOURCES UNKNOWN.*

Hear the plea of our souls
Sent after you in trust:
We need here for our earthly work
Strong power from spirit-lands

For One who took His Own Life

✦ From *MANTRISCHE SPRÜCHE SEELENÜBUNGEN II*, p. 228.

Soul in the land of souls,
Seek the mercy of the Christ,
That will bring you help,
The help from spirit lands
That gives peace also
To those spirits
Who will despair
Of life without peace.

✦ From *TRUTH-WROUGHT-WORDS*, p. 91.

May my love be interwoven,
As my heart's offering,
In the sheaths that now surround you,
Cooling all your heat,
Warming all your cold.
Live — love-upborne,
Light-rayed-through — Gift of light, on upward!

✦ From *MEDITATIVE POETRY OF RUDOLF STEINER*, Spring Valley, NY: Mercury Press, 1991. Translations by William Gardner, edited by Malcolm Gardner & Lydia Wieder, p. 2. [(GA 268), p. 215, Archive #3412.]

May love follow you, soul,
Who lives yonder in spirit,
Who gazes at earth life;
Encountering itself as spirit.
And may that which appears to you in soul-land
As your own thinking self
Accept our love,
So that we may feel ourselves in you,
And you may find in our soul
That which lives with you in devotion.

At the Death of a Student

✦ From *Towards the Deepening of Waldorf Education: Excerpts of the Work of Rudolf Steiner — Essays and Documents*, Dornach: Verlag am Goetheanum, 1991, p. 120.

You were given to us
By your parents' will
That you might enter strongly
Into future earth lives.

So take with you,
Instead of school's guidance
For earthly action and life,
The loving thoughts of the teacher
Beyond to that spirit-existence,

In the pain at the threshold of death
Only the winged words of soul
May be spoken that determine
A ripening life.

Where the soul is woven through
With the bright light of eternity
And the spirit experiences
The aim of God's will.

The Foundation Stone Verse

of the Anthroposophical Society   by Helmut von Kügelgen

On New Year's Eve of 1922 the first Goetheanum burned down. The arson that destroyed this building destroyed a work of art, for in it Rudolf Steiner had artistically placed his lifework before the world. Rudolf Steiner's response to this blow of destiny, which robbed him of enormous life forces that could not be replaced, was to continue his work at an even higher level of intensity. He gave and he gave out of the fullness of his spiritual creativity. The year 1923 thus passed in a tireless series of lectures, travels, and founding of new initiatives. The crowning of the year was the Christmas Foundation Meeting of 1923/24, during which the General Anthroposophical Society was newly founded.

It was to be the freest society, free of all sectarian and cliquish concerns, so that anyone could join it, without regard to nationality, race or religious affiliation. The only requirement was that one felt it right that a place exist, such as the Goetheanum in Dornach, to carry on research and inner schooling out of Spiritual Science. Rudolf Steiner placed himself into this newly founded Society, uniting himself with the destiny of the members by serving as General Secretary.

Those of us working and living with the art of education that has arisen from his work should know that to this work there also belongs the unique social and community form of the Society founded at the Christmas Foundation Meeting. He placed the Foundation Stone of this Society in the hearts of the members — that is the following mantra with its four parts. Day after day during the Christmas Foundation Meeting, Rudolf Steiner spoke verses from the Foundation Stone Mantra, and for each day he wrote a "Rhythm" on the blackboard. At the end of this section these rhythms are written, and one can work with them as an exercise each day of the week, thereby uniting oneself with this social deed of Rudolf Steiner's.

Further reading on the Foundation Stone:

- THE CHRISTMAS CONFERENCE FOR THE FOUNDATION OF THE GENERAL ANTHROPOSOPHICAL SOCIETY, 1923/24, Anthroposophic Press, (1990).
- THE FOUNDATION STONE, Zeylmans von Emichhofen, Rudolf Steiner Press, London, (1963).
- PATH TO AN UNDERSTANDING OF THE FOUNDATION STONE MEDITATION, Ernst Katz and Rene Querido, Anthroposophical Society in America, (1997).

of the General Anthroposophical Society

25 December 1923 at 10:00 a.m.

A note on the following translations: Most of the passages from Rudolf Steiner's talks are taken from the English version of THE PROCEEDINGS OF THE CHRISTMAS CONFERENCE, Anthroposophic Press, (1990), although a few sections have been newly translated. The translation of the Foundation Stone itself was developed by speech artists in North America.

Dr. Steiner greeted those present with the following words:

My dear friends! Let the first words that resound through this room today be those which sum up the essence of what may stand before your souls as the most important findings of recent years.

Later there will be more to be said about these words which are, as they stand, a summary. But first let our ears be touched by them, so that out of the signs of the present time we may renew, in keeping with our way of thinking, the ancient word of the Mysteries: "Know thyself."

Human soul!
You live within the limbs
Which bears you through the world of space
Into the spirit's ocean-being:
Practice spirit-recalling
In depths of soul,
Where in the wielding
World-Creator-Being
Your own I
Comes into being
In the I of God;
And you will truly live
In human world-all being.

Human soul!
You live within the beat of heart and lung
Which leads you through the rhythms of time
Into the feeling of your own soul-being:

of the General Anthroposophical Society

Practice spirit-sensing
In the balance of the soul,
Where the surging deeds
Of world-evolving
Unite your own I
With the I of the world;
And you will truly feel
In human soul's creating.

Human soul!
You live within the resting head
Which forms the grounds of eternity
Unlocks for you world-thoughts:
Practice spirit-beholding
In stillness of thought,
Where the god's eternal aims
Bestow the light of cosmic being
On your own I
For free and active willing.
And you will truly think
In human spirit depths.

My dear friends! Today when I look back specifically to what it was possible to bring from the spiritual worlds while the terrible storms of war were surging across the earth, I find it all expressed as though in a paradigm in the trio of verses your ears have just heard.

For decades it has been possible to perceive this threefoldness of man that enables him in the wholeness of his being of spirit, soul and body to revive for himself once more in a new form the call, "Know thyself." For decades it has been possible to perceive this threefoldness. But only in the last decade have I myself been able to bring it to full maturity while the storms of war were raging. I sought to indicate how the human being lives in the physical realm in the metabolic system and the limbs, in the rhythmic system of heart and lungs, and in the system of thinking and perceiving with the head. Yesterday I indicated how this threefoldness can be rightly taken up when our hearts are enlivened through and through by Anthroposophia.

We may be sure that if man learns to know in his feeling and in his will what he is actually doing, when, as the spirits of the universe enliven him, he lets his limbs place him in the world of space, not in a suffering, passive grasping of the universe but in an active grasping of the world in which he fulfills his duties, his tasks, his mission on the earth — then in this active grasping of the world he will know the being of all-wielding love of man and universe which is one member of the all-world-being.

We may be sure that if mankind understands the miraculous mystery holding sway between lung and heart — expressing inwardly the best of universal rhythms working across millennia, across the eons of time to ensoul humanity with the universe through the rhythms of pulse and blood — we may hope that, grasping this in wisdom with a heart that has become a sense organ, mankind can experience the divinely given universal images as out of themselves they actively reveal the cosmos. Just as in active movement we grasp the all-wielding love of worlds, so shall we grasp the archetypal images of world existence when we sense in ourselves the mysterious interplay between universal rhythm and heart rhythm, and through this the human rhythm that takes place mysteriously in soul and spirit realms in the interplay between lung and heart.

And when, in feeling, the human being rightly perceives what is revealed in the system of his head, which is at rest on his shoulders even when he walks along, then, feeling himself within the system of his head and pouring warmth of heart into this system of his head, he will experience the ruling, working, weaving thoughts of the universe within his own being.

Thus he becomes the threefoldness of all existence: universal love reigning in human love; universal imagination reigning in the forms of the human organism; universal thoughts reigning mysteriously below the surface in human thoughts. He will grasp this threefoldness and he will recognize himself as an individually free human being within the reigning work of the gods in the cosmos, as a cosmic human being, an individual human being within the cosmic human being, working for the future of the universe as an individual human being within the cosmic human being. Out of the signs of the present time he will re-enliven the ancient words: "Know thou thyself!"

The Greeks were still permitted to omit the final word, since for them the human self was not yet as abstract as it is for us now that it has become concentrated in the abstract ego-point or at most in thinking, feeling and willing. For them human nature comprised the totality of spirit, soul and body. Thus the ancient Greeks were permitted to believe that they spoke of the total human being, spirit, soul and body, when they let resound the ancient word of the Sun, the word of Apollo: "Know thou thyself!"

Today, re-enlivening these words in the right way out of the signs of our times, we have to say, "Soul of man, know thou thyself in the weaving existence of spirit, soul and body," When we say this, we have understood what lies at the foundation of all aspects of the being of man. In the substance of the universe there is and works and lives the spirit which streams from the heights and reveals itself in the human head; the force of Christ working in the circumference, weaving in the air, encircling the earth, works and lives in the system of our breath; and from the inmost depths of the earth rise up the forces which work in our limbs. When now, at this moment, we unite these three forces, the forces of the heights, the forces of the circumference, the forces of the depths, in a substance that gives form, then in the understanding of our soul we can bring face to face the universal dodecahedron with the human dodecachedron. Out of these three forces: out of the spirit of the heights, out of the force of Christ in the circumference, out of the working of the Father, the creative activity of the Father that streams out of the depths, let us at this moment give into the soil of our souls so that it may remain there a powerful sign in the foundations of our soul existence and so that in the future working of the Anthroposophical Society we may stand on this firm Foundation Stone.

Let us ever remain aware of this Foundation Stone for the Anthroposophical Society, formed today. In all that we shall do, in the outer world and here, to further, to develop and to fully unfold the Anthroposophical Society, let us preserve the remembrance of the Foundation Stone which we have today lowered into the soil of our hearts. Let us seek in the threshold being of man, which teaches us love, which teaches us the universal imagination, which teaches us the universal thoughts; let us seek, in this threefold being, the substance of universal love which we lay as the foundation, let us seek in this threefold being the archetype of the imagination according to which we shape the universal love within our hearts, let us seek the power of thoughts from the heights which enable us to let shine forth in fitting manner this dodecahedral imagination which has received its form through love! Then shall we carry away with us from here what we need. Then shall the Foundation Stone shine forth before the eyes of our soul, that Foundation Stone which has received its substance from universal love and human love, its picture image, its form, from universal imagination and human imagination, and its brilliant radiance from universal thoughts and human thoughts, its brilliant radiance which, whenever we recollect this moment can shine towards us with warm light, with light that spurs on our deeds, our thinking, our feeling and our willing.

The proper soil into which we must lower the Foundation Stone of today, the proper soil consists of our hearts in their harmonious collaboration, in their good, love-filled desire to bear together the will of anthroposophy through the world. This will cast its light on us like a reminder of the light of thought that can ever shine towards us from the dodecahedral stone of love that today we will lower into our hearts.

Dear friends, let us take this deeply into our souls. With it let us warm our souls, and with it let us enlighten our souls. Let us cherish this warmth of soul and this light of soul that out of good will we have planted in our hearts today.

We plant it, my dear friends, at a moment when human memory that truly understands the universe looks back to the point in human evolution, at the turning point of time, when out of the darkness of night and out of the darkness of human moral feeling, shooting like light from heaven, was born the divine being who had become the Christ, the spirit being who had entered into humankind.

We can best bring strength to that warmth of soul and that light of soul which we need, if we enliven them with the warmth and the light that shone forth at the turning point of time as the Light of Christ in the darkness of the universe. In our hearts, in our thoughts and in our will let us bring to life that original consecrated night of Christmas which took place two thousand years ago, so that it may help us when we carry forth into the world what shines towards us through the light of thought of that dodecahedral Foundation Stone of love which is shaped in accordance with the universe and has been laid into the human realm. So let the feelings of our hearts be turned back towards the original consecrated night of Christmas in ancient Palestine.

At the turning point of time
The spirit-light of the world
Entered the stream of earth existence.
Darkness of night
Had ceased its reign,
Day-radiant light
Shone forth in human souls:
Light
That gives warmth
To simple shepherds' hearts;
Light
That enlightens
The wise heads of kings.

Light divine,
Christ-Sun,
Warm
Our hearts;
Enlighten
Our heads;
That good may become
What from our hearts
We are founding,
What from our heads
We direct,
With focused will.

The turning of our feelings back to the original consecrated night of Christmas can give us the strength of the warming of our hearts and the enlightening of our heads which we need if we are to practice rightly, working anthroposophically, what can arise from the knowledge of the threefold human being coming to harmony in unity.

So let us once more gather before our souls all that follows from a true understanding of the words, "Know thou thyself in spirit, soul and body." Let us gather it as it works in the cosmos so that to our Foundation Stone, which we have now laid in the soil of our hearts, there may speak from everywhere into human existence and into human life and into human work everything that the universe has to say to this human existence and to this human life and to this human work.

Human soul!
You live within the limbs
Which bear you through the world of space
Into the spirit's ocean-being:
Practice spirit-recalling
In depths of soul,
Where in the wielding
World-Creator-Being
Your own I
Comes into being
In the I of God;
And you will truly live
In human world--all being.

For the Father-Spirit of the heights holds sway
In depths of worlds begetting life.
Spirits of Strength:
Let ring forth from the heights
What in the depths is echoed,
Speaking:
Out of the Godhead we are born,
This is heard by the spirits of the elements

The Laying of the Foundation Stone

of the General Anthroposophical Society

In east, west, north, south:
May human beings hear it!

Human Soul!
You live within the beat of heart and lung
Which leads you through the rhythms of time
Into the feeling of your own soul-being:
Practice spirit-sensing
In balance of the soul,
Where the surging deeds
Of world-evolving
Unite your own I
With the I of the world;
And you will truly feel
In human soul's creating.

For the Christ-will encircling us holds sway.
In world rhythms,
Bestowing grace upon souls.
Spirits of Light:
Let from the east be enkindled
What through the west takes on form,
Speaking:
In Christ death becomes life.
This is heard by the spirits of the elements
In east, west, north, south:
May human beings hear it!

Human soul!
You live within the resting head
Which from the grounds of eternity
Unlocks for your world-thoughts:
Practice spirit-beholding
In stillness of thought,
Where the gods' eternal aims

of the General Anthroposophical Society

Bestow the light of cosmic being
On your own I
For free and active willing.
And you will truly think
In human spirit depths.

For the Spirit's world-thoughts hold sway
In cosmic being, imploring light.
Spirits of Soul:
Let from the depths be entreated
What in the heights will be heard,
Speaking:
In the Spirit's cosmic thoughts the soul awakens.
This is heard by the spirits of the elements
In east, west, north, south:
May human beings hear it!

My dear friends, hear it as it resounds in your own hearts! Then you will found here a true community of human beings for Anthroposophia, and then will you carry the spirit that rules in the shining light of thoughts around the dodecahedral Stone of love out into the world wherever it should give of its light and of its warmth for the progress of human souls, for the progress of the universe.

From the Talk on Wednesday, 26 December 1923

We can see in the content of the given statutes that we must connect the greatest openness with the Anthroposophical Society. My dear friends, the times do not allow for anything else to arise. Everything that sinks into something secretive cannot be carried by the present times. It is this that gives us a fundamental problem that we must resolve. I do not mean, that we will have to spend our time during this conference debating, but rather we must resolve this fundamental problem in our hearts. We need to be perfectly clear that in our Society there is just this task of uniting together the greatest openness we can think of with a true esoteric.

Yes, my dear friends, we have experienced the demonstration of this problem from all sides, first through the obstacles and hindrances of the terrible war, and then also through the various internal difficulties with which we have had to live.

Essentially there were no gatherings of the Anthroposophical Society in recent times that did not have just this problem in the background, although few may have noticed it. The problem is how to unite the fullest openness with the deepest, most serious, most inward esoteric. It is therefore essential that in all of our gatherings in the future we be certain to rise beyond that which is normally called organizational matters. Anthroposophy does not need the organizational in the usual sense of the word. Where anthroposophy finds a true understanding in the heart, then those hearts will ring together, without heads knocking against one another. And if we can solve this purely human problem and help hearts to beat together without heads knocking against one another, then from the human side we will have done everything possible to accomplish those things indicated here, even in the leadership of the Anthroposophical Society.

And we must accomplish this so that in all of our actions we have a feeling for the cooperative working of the spiritual world for this is exactly the difference between the Anthroposophical Society and some other organization that may exist at this time. The difference must be that out of the power of anthroposophy itself the possibility exists that the greatest openness imaginable be connected to the truest, most inward esoteric. And the esoteric will not fail us in the future, even in our activities. In this realm we must learn what we can from the events of the last ten years. . .that which we must find is this: We stand as a small society in relation to the world, and the world — you know of what I am referring — does not actually love us. That is a fact that we cannot alter. But we do not need to do anything extra to make ourselves even more unloved. I do not mean this in a trivial sense. Rather I mean it in the deepest sense, which is really spoken out of the foundation of occult life. We do not need to ask ourselves again and again what we should do in regard to this or that circle which does not love us at this time.

How must we conduct ourselves in this or that realm so that we will be fully accepted when in our activity we feel at every moment that we are responsible to the spiritual world, when we really know that the spiritual world wants to do something with human evolution at this historical time. It wants to do something in various realms of life, and it is clear and true to us that we need to follow these impulses that come from the spiritual world. Even if this gives us a shock at first, it is this that will eventually bring healing. And therefore we will only come to rights with ourselves if we take every opportunity to permeate ourselves with that which comes as an impulse from the spiritual world.

The Concluding Talk on 1 January 1924 at 8:30 a.m.

With thoughts that are not easy but which are grave we must depart from this Conference that has led to the founding of the General Anthroposophical Society. But I do not think it will be necessary for anybody to go away with pessimism from what has taken place here this Christmas. Every day we have had to walk past the sad ruins of the Goetheanum. But as we have walked up this hill, past these ruins, I think that in every soul there has also been the content of what has been discussed here and what has quite evidently been understood by our friends in their hearts. From all this, the thought has emerged: It will be possible for spiritual flames of fire to arise, as a true spiritual life for the blessing of mankind in the future, from the Goetheanum which is built anew. They shall arise out of our hard work and out of our devotion. The more we go from here with the courage to carry on the affairs of Anthroposophy, the better have we heard the breath of the spirit wafting again and again through our gathering, filled with hope. For the scene I have described to you, and which can be seen so frequently, the scene of present-day human beings, the products of a decadent civilization and education, approaching the Guardian of the Threshold in a state of sleep, is actually not one that is found amongst the circle of sensitive anthroposophists. Here, on the whole, the circumstance is such that only a warning, one particular exhortation, resounds: In hearing the voice from the land of the spirit you must develop the strong courage to bear witness to this voice, for you have begun to awaken; courage will keep you awake; lack of courage alone could lead you to fall asleep.

My dear friends, yesterday was the anniversary of the day on which we saw the tongues of flame devouring our old Goetheanum. Today we may hope — since a year ago we did not allow even the flames to distract us from continuing with our work — that when the physical Goetheanum stands here once more we shall have worked in such a way that the physical Goetheanum is only the external symbol for our spiritual Goetheanum which we want to take with us as an idea as we now go out into the world.

We have here laid the Foundation Stone. On this Foundation Stone shall be erected the building whose individual stones will be the work achieved in all our groups by the individuals outside in the wide world. Let us now look in spirit at this work and become conscious of the responsibility about which I have spoken today, of our responsibility towards the human being standing before the Guardian of the Threshold who has to be refused entry into the spiritual world. Certainly it should never occur to us to feel anything but the deepest pain and the deepest sorrow for that which occurred here a year ago. But everything in the world, of that we can also be certain, that has achieved a certain magnitude is born out of such pain. And so may our pain be so turned, that from it a strong, glowing Anthroposophic Society can arise through your work, my dear friends.

Towards these aims we have deepened ourselves with those words with which I have begun, with those words with which I want to close this Christmas Conference, which is a time of consecration,[3] a festival of consecration for us not only for the beginning of a new year, but for a beginning of a turning point in time, to which we want to dedicate ourselves with a devotion-filled tending of the spiritual life:

Human soul!
You live within the limbs
Which bear you through the world of space
Into the spirit's ocean-being:
Practice spirit-recalling
Where in the wielding
World-Creator-Being
Your own I
Comes into being
In the I of God;
And you will truly live

In human world-all being.
For the Father-Spirit of the heights holds sway
In depths of worlds begetting life.
Spirits of Strength:
Let ring forth from the heights
What in the depths is echoed,
Speaking:
Out of the Godhead we are born.
This is heard by the spirits of the elements
In east, west, north, south:
May human beings hear it!

Human soul!
You live within the beat of heart and lung
Which leads you through the rhythms of time
Into the feeling of your own soul-being:
Practice spirit-sensing
In balance of the soul,
Where the surging deeds
Of world-evolving
Unite your own I
With the I of the World;
And you will truly feel
In human soul's creating.

For the Christ-will encircling us holds sway,
In world rhythms, bestowing grace upon souls.
Spirits of Light:
Let from the east be enkindled
What through the west takes on form,
Speaking:
In Christ death becomes life
This is heard by the spirits of the elements
In east, west, north, south:
May human beings hear it!

of the General Anthroposophical Society

Human soul!
You live within the resting head
Which from the grounds of eternity
Unlocks for you world-thoughts:
Practice spirit-beholding
In stillness of thought,
Where the gods' eternal aims
Bestow the light of cosmic being
On your own I
For free and active willing.
And you will truly think
In human spirit depths.

For the Spirit's world-thoughts hold sway
In cosmic being, imploring light.
Spirits of Soul:
Let from the depths be entreated
What in the heights will be heard,
Speaking:
In the Spirit's cosmic thoughts the soul awakens.
This is heard by the spirits of the elements
In east, west, north, south:
May human beings hear it!

At the turning point of time
The Spirit-light of the world
Entered the stream of earth existence.
Darkness of night
Had ceased its reign;
Day-radiant light
Shone forth in human souls:
Light
That gives warmth
To simple shepherds' hearts;
Light
That enlightens
The wise heads of kings.

Light divine,
Christ-Sun,
Warm
Our hearts;
Enlighten
Our heads;
That good may become
What from our hearts
We are founding,
What from our heads
We direct,
With focused will

And so, my dear friends,[4] bear out with you into the world your warm hearts in whose soil you have laid the Foundation Stone for the Anthroposophical Society, bear out with you your warm hearts in order to do work in the world that is strong in healing. Help will come to you because your heads will be enlightened by what you all now want to be able to direct in conscious willing. Let us today make this resolve with all our strength. And we shall see that if we show ourselves to be worthy, then a good star will shine over that which is willed from here. My dear friends, follow this good star. We shall see whither the gods shall lead us through the light of this star. ❖

Light divine,
Christ-Sun,
Warm
Our hearts;
Enlighten
Our heads!

WEDNESDAY

Spirit-recalling
Your own I
Comes into being
In the I of God

Spirit-sensing
Unite your own I
With the I
of the World

Spirit-beholding
Bestow your own I
For free and active
willing

THURSDAY

Your own I
Comes into being
In the I of God

Unite your own I
With the I
of the World

Bestow on your own I
For free and active
willing

Live
In human
world-all being

Feel
In human soul's
creating

Think
In human spirit depths

FRIDAY

Practice spirit-recalling
For the Father-Spirit
Of the heights
holds sway

Practice spirit-sensing
For the Christ-will
encircling us
holds sway

Practice spirit-beholding
For the Spirit's
world-thoughts
hold sway

In depths of worlds
begetting life

In world rhythms
bestowing grace
upon souls

In cosmic being
imploring light

SATURDAY [5]

Practice beholding | Practice spirit-sensing | Practice spirit-recalling

Spirits of Strength
Let ring forth from
the heights
What in the depths
is echoed.

Spirits of Light
Let from the east
be enkindled
What through the
west takes on form.

Spirits of Soul
Let from the depths
be enkindled
What in the heights
will be heard

(One speaks:
*Ex Deo Nascimur
Sanctum*
Out of the Godhead
we are born.)

(One speaks:
*In Christo
Morimur.*
In Christ, death
becomes life.)

(One speaks:
*Per Spiritum Sanctum
reviviscimus.*
In the Spirit's cosmic
thoughts the soul awakens.)

SUNDAY

Practice
spirit-sensing

Practice
spirit-recalling

That good may become
What from our hearts
We are foundling,
What from our heads
We direct,
With focused will.

Practice
spirit-beholding

MONDAY

Light divine,
Christ-Sun!
This is heard by the spirits
of the elements
In east, west, north, south
May human beings hear it!

TUESDAY

You live within
the limbs

You live within
the beat of heart & lung

You live within
the resting head

For the Father-Spirit
Of the heights
holds sway

For the Christ-will
encircling us
holds sway

For the Spirit's
world-thoughts
hold sway

In depths of worlds
Begetting life

In world rhythms,
bestowing grace
upon souls

In cosmic being,
imploring light

Foundation Stone Meditation:
Threefoldness and the Fourth Element

(This article was originally written as an introduction to the booklet, PATH TO AN UNDERSTANDING OF THE FOUNDATION STONE MEDITATION, published by the Anthroposophical Society in America, and is included here in a modified form after conversations with Dr. von Kügelgen.)

One of the beautiful aspects of the Foundation Stone meditation is the picture it gives of the human being and the relationship of the threefold soul of the human I or ego. The meditation addresses the human soul and shows how the soul lives in the threefold nature of the human being: In the bodily organization of the limbs, the heart and lungs, and the resting head; in the soul forces of thinking, feeling and willing; and in the spirit world of the Trinity, called here the Father-spirit, the Christ-will, and the Spirit-thoughts. Rudolf Steiner spent many years of his life forming the threefold picture of the human being in lectures and books, but nowhere does it resound quite as strongly as in the Foundation Stone. The mantric power of its verses allows this rich human picture to enter deeply into our being. This picture can help to counter the popular images of the human being that tend, on the one hand, to inflate our stature or, on the other, to diminish us.

An additional aspect of the mystery and power of the Foundation Stone meditation is that it goes much further than the traditional view of the threefold nature of the human soul and shows the relationship of the human soul to a fourth element, the ego or I. When Rudolf Steiner speaks of the threefold nature of the human being in his lectures, there is an implied understanding that the threefold development is but a preparation for the incarnation of the I. However, since the ego's activity is not always expressly stated, one could have the impression that the threefold nature of the individual represents the complete human being.

Two pictures of child's development may help to clarify the relationship of the I to the human being's threefold nature. One picture pertains to the first three years of life when the child learns to walk, to talk and to think. These deeds relate to the will realm, the rhythmic or feeling realm, and the thinking realm respectively. What marks the end of this three-year period is the child's first recognition of self. Around the age of three, the child begins to call itself, "I." This momentous event points to the intimate relationship between the threefold nature of the human being and the I.

Threefoldness and the Fourth Element

Another picture of the child's development encompasses the first twenty-one years. In the first seven years the emphasis is on the development of will; in the elementary school years, on feeling; and in the last seven, on thinking. The young person's development is not complete, however, until the birth of the I, which takes place around the age of twenty-one. At this age the period of self-education begins, as the ego makes its own decisions in freedom.

From these pictures of childhood and youth, a clearer image of the full nature of the human being can arise. The individual develops in a threefold way but is not complete without the I. A threefold human being without an ego is hollow. Outwardly it may seem complete, just as a warm, humanistic picture of the human being with its emphasis on body and soul can seem complete, but inwardly there would be a terrible void. Without the spiritual force of the I bringing continual renewal, the soul forces of thinking, feeling and willing would gradually stagnate and begin to fall apart, much as the body does after death, when the I has receded.

If the development of the first twenty-one years is able to proceed normally and if the I is able to incarnate around that age, then the individual is well-prepared for further growth in the adult years. Having fully developed the physical body in the first twenty-one years, he or she is able to deepen the soul forces between twenty-one and forty-two and the spiritual forces between forty-two and sixty-three.

It seems that so many adults today have an imbalance in their threefold nature. Is there a way to heal this imbalance while striving towards spiritual development? One way is through regularly working with the Foundation Stone that has a healing power through its capacity to address the human soul in its threefold nature and call it into a balanced whole. When one works with the rhythms of the meditation each day, and also works with the whole meditation from time to time, one experiences recognition of one's full human nature. Its first three panels call to the human soul to find a true relationship to willing, feeling and thinking, and working with the meditation daily has a harmonizing, beneficial effect on the threefold nature of the soul. The fourth panel speaks especially to the I, relating to the Christ Being who stands as a higher image of the I. Thus, in its structure of three parallel panels with a very different fourth panel, the Foundation Stone meditation mirrors the threefold human being with the I as a fourth element.

Threefoldness and the Fourth Element

The fourth panel brings a whole new mood into the meditation. This change in mood is evident when one sees the Foundation Stone done in the eurythmy form created by Rudolf Steiner. There are strong parallels in the way that the first three panels are presented. The eurythmists wear the same deep colored garments for each of the three verses, which are separated from one another only by a moment of darkness on the stage. At the end of the third panel, however, the eurythmists slowly leave the stage, which remains empty for a time. When they return dressed in gold and white, the entire mood and the movements are very different from those of the first three verses.

In the forth panel one feel something new has entered. Although this panel refers to the turning point of time and of the Christ's relationship to the shepherds and the kings, one nevertheless feels that it is speaking of the Logos as it can be experienced today. It reminds me of Rudolf Steiner's sculpture of the Representative of Humanity and also of his descriptions of Christ in the etheric world. There is something very modern and contemporary about the Being of the fourth panel, reminiscent of the description given by individuals meeting the Christ, especially in near-death experiences. They often speak of a being of light with tremendous capacities of warmth and love. Some call this being the Christ, but others have no name for it. Only once in this fourth panel is the Being called the Christ and then it is "Christ-Sun." It is as if Rudolf Steiner is seeking a new way to describe this Being, and again and again he uses the words "light," "warmth" and "enlighten."

After this tremendous picture of the Christ as Being of the Sun, the final lines of the verse change in tone and bring us back to earth again. This is important, for there are many people who feel the light of the Christ but then yearn for loftier and loftier realms of light so that in the end they enter Lucifer's light-filled realm, rather than remaining in Christ's realm of love and compassion. In this verse, after calling upon the light-filled forces of the Christ, Rudolf Steiner calls us back to our own threefold, balanced nature so that head and heart can work together with focused will. Then human beings may work together, and goodness may become part of life again.

Threefoldness and the Fourth Element

The structure of the Foundation Stone Meditation is beautiful and stands like a higher picture of the human being: a threefold nature crowned by the I that is filled with the light of the Christ. With such a picture in mind one can understand the Pauline words, "Not I, but the Christ in me." They are not meant as a negation of the I, but a fulfillment of the I as it finds its completion in the Being of the Christ. ❖

by Joan Almon

Endnote 1 — page 43

The point here is not the extent to which any particular natural scientific view can or cannot find these thoughts justifiable. The point is to develop thoughts about plants and human beings that can be acquired by means of simple, direct observation without any theory whatsoever. These thoughts do have a value alongside other, more theoretical ideas (which are no less valuable in other respects) about things in the outer world. In this case, the purpose of these thoughts is not to present facts in a scientific way, but to build up a symbol that proves effective on a soul level, regardless of whatever objections may occur to one or the other individual as it is being built up. — R. Steiner

Endnote 2 — page 44

How to Know Higher Worlds: A Modern Path of Initiation, Anthroposophic Press, Hudson, NY, 1994.

Endnote 3 —— page 64

Here Rudolf Steiner speaks of a "Weihenacht" festival, a time of consecration, which is a similar word in German to the Weilnacht festival, the Christmas festival which he refers to in the same sentence.

Endnote 4 — page 67

In the closing sentences of the Christmas Foundation Meeting as in the opening, Rudolf Steiner changed from the formal mode of address to the more intimate "Du."

Endnote 5 — page 69

What is indicated in the Saturday rhythm in parentheses was not written on the blackboard by Rudolf Steiner during the Christmas Conference as being part of the rhythm. The connection to the Rosicrucian words was first indicated in the German language when the mantra appeared publicly for the first time in print on 13 January 1924. Small variations in the text, in punctuation for instance, appeared already during the Christmas Conference. Rudolf Steiner was continually working to bring spiritual content into the world — and as an exercise we must continue to re–experience the spiritual power of the word and to ensheath the word again with that power. (Helmut von Kügelgen). Translated by the Speech Association of North America.